CHRONICLES OF A BROKEN HEART.....

BOOK OF POETRY BY

RESTORATION OF THE BREACH
WITHOUT BORDERS

EVOL "JUVIE" DILLON

CHRONICLES OF A BROKEN HEART

ISBN: 978-1-954755-31-4

Published by:

Restoration of the Breach without Borders

West Palm Beach, Florida 33407

restorativeauthor@gmail.com

Tele: (561) 388-2949

Cover Design by:

EVOL DILLON

Formatting and Publishing done

by:

Leostone Morrison

Publisher.20@aol.com

"Heartbreaks are hard to deal with but you have to just brush off and keep moving

because life never stops and waits for you, the clock always keeps ticking."

-Juvie

Author's note

It was a warm afternoon in 1995, when I was summoned to the offices of The Transport Authority, 119 Maxfield Avenue, Kingston, Jamaica W.I. the place where my mother had been employed for so many years. I can't remember the exact month or the day it was almost 24 years ago, all I can recall was the disappointment in my mother's voice when she called and said that my English teacher had informed her that I was not being recommended to sit the CXC English Language exam. I knew English was not one of my strong points, so I had already planned for failing anyway. Upon arrival I was greeted somewhat nonchalantly as was expected in light of the circumstances, I was told by her "Commander MacFarlane wants to speak to you". I nodded my head as I was escorted by her to the office of the Managing Director. She knocked on the door and a voice said "enter" and as we did there sat a beautiful lady by the name of Teena Miller, she beckoned me to go and sit in the office stating that he was in a meeting and would be with me shortly.

After what seemed like an eternity and a lot of murmuring and wondering what kind of lecture about my schoolwork was coming that would fall on deaf ears as I had already decided that selling drugs is the only way to get rich, in stepped this man with this big smile and bright personality. I was wondering why he was so friendly towards me, especially since we were strangers (little did I know this talk would change my life forever). We chatted about football and how much I wanted to play and how good his son was and Rastafarianism and Christianity. It was there and then that reality struck me and I started to see the bigger picture that there was more to life than just money, flashy cars, pretty girls, designer clothes and all the other material things. He introduced me to a book titled "English Made Simple" and taught me the art of effective communications and literary devices and metaphors, then I started to visit his office twice a week for English classes and it was there that my love for writing was born.

Acknowledgements

"I am grateful to all the people who played a role in my life"

First and foremost, ***Audrey Johnson*** my loving mother, words can't express my gratitude, you know my story and you are the main character in the plot of things. My two sons Khalfani and Hasani love you endlessly, my sisters Gail and Tracey we share a bond like no other, the mother of my children Calecia and Sophia (I know the stress I put you both through). My uncle Christopher, you taught me the value of people versus the value of things and that nothing is too good to share with others. My aunt Michelle (my favorite aunt without apology), my cousin Shenequa (my favorite again) my other mothers Audrey Smith-Facey, Arlene Barnes, Denise Daley and, my stepfather Mr. Cole you were the first father I knew and you raised me like your own child, I'm forever grateful. My father Junior Dillon, you played your part (better late than never). To my mentor Commander John MacFarlane, the man who I owe a lot, you inspired my love for reading and writing. To the other members of my family too much to mention.......

My fellow poets and writers, the special people who keep me writing Nadia, Tamara, Sasha, Kiki, Marvin, Julien, Marcus and all the rest....

Last and not least all my "boobies", all my social media friends... To Carol, my aunt in law who was the first to contribute to the cause... I just want to say how much I appreciate every single deed, be it large or small...

Foreword

This book "Chronicles Of A Broken Heart" is a deep introspective expression of the rollercoaster of emotions that comes with human relations and interactions.

It takes you on a journey inside the pages of hurt and the strength it takes to maneuver the healing process. The relatability of the material makes some portions of it a bit heartbreaking but worth reading every page and the outpouring of emotions is something we all can relate to but maybe never expressed in this manner.

" Chronicles Of A Broken Heart" is liberating and awakening for us to be authentic in our journaling to healing.

Pamela D. Redwood: Former Executive Adviser to former Prime Minister of Jamaica- Most Hon. Portia Simpson Miller

Table Of Contents

INTRODUCTION

Poetry is defined as “literary work in which special intensity is given to the expression of feelings and ideas by use of distinctive style and rhythm; collectively or as a genre of literature”. That being said, two of the strongest feelings to be expressed are joys and sorrows. Sharing joy is a great feeling and one not to be underestimated at face value because it is vital to the human psyche, and it is a very effective medicine for stress relief and likewise sorrows are a contributing factor to the aforementioned.

Different people have different ways of dealing with situations that may arise from time to time but one thing for sure is that it is best to get it out of your system by whatever means you find most comfortable or whatever works for you. Some people do it through physical activity, reading, eating, drinking, smoking, partying, talking about it or other forms. I express my thoughts best through my writing. When my pen touches paper or my fingers hit that keyboard it's like I'm in a trance, I’m in this zone that I just keep flowing until I’m finished. Over the years I have written several hundred poems and some are from my own personal experiences and others are from persons relating their experiences to me and also just from looking at life and seeing the things that happen sometimes.

This book "Chronicles Of A Broken Heart" is a collection of poems relating to bad experiences and I'm sure that almost every human being will have their heart broken at some stage of life but it is most definitely not the end of loving and I hope that these poems that are written about these experiences will not only give some comfort to know that you are not alone or your situation is not unique but that this is the real world and these things happen. It is not about dwelling on the past but more about letting go of what you endured and growing stronger from the lessons learnt.

I've been writing poems for over 12 years now. As much as it may not seem like all that long when compared to other writers, I have come a far way. This book "Chronicles Of A Broken Heart" is my first venture out into the publishing world (after a lot of persuasion) and I hold it dear to my heart because a lot of these poems were written when I was at an emotionally low point in my life and also some of them are based on heart to heart conversations I have had with some of my friends and even just people who felt comfortable enough to pour their emotions into the cup of a stranger.

For this I am forever grateful and here I am pouring out their stories, my stories and hopefully they become your stories…

÷ Apology To My Heart *÷*

We all make mistakes in life sometimes and you should
never be too big to recognize.

The ultimate form of humility is recognition and apology,
never be too big to apologize.

Saying sorry for your mistakes may not mend broken
relationships but it's the first step.

Emotionally draining while you sleep, your actions affecting
below the surface, in depth.

Inept and unconscionable factions not caring about the
repercussions of your actions.

Recklessly and selfishly thinking of your own desires and dividing emotions into fractions.

Doing as you please, evincing a roller coaster of feelings, with not even a worry.

Now it's time to recognize and apologize, you can never be too big to say that you are sorry.

I apologize for all the pain and hurt I put you through…

You are the one who feels the pains for the stupid things I do…

Negative energies are sometimes so very kinetic and magnetic...

It's hard to explain and you may not get it, still I'm apologetic…

It was never my intention to cause you hurt and pain, I was just seeking love at the start.

Now through my own indulgence I may have caused irreparable damage to my own heart.

Enjoying the now moments, and not thinking about the repercussions of later.

Instantaneously gratification takes precedence over the karma which is greater.

No refrain, thinking only of the joys that I can momentarily enjoy and all there is to gain.

Not for a moment thinking about the long-term effect, the sorrows to come and all the pain.

Ignorance is bliss, I am fool to my lust, blind indulgence my forte', wanting all I can get.

Adept at Ignoring the next step and aftereffects, trying to connect, now living in regret.

I apologize for all the pain and hurt I put you through…

You are the one who feels the pains for the stupid things I do…

Negative energies are sometimes so very kinetic and magnetic...

It's hard to explain and you may not get it, still I'm apologetic…

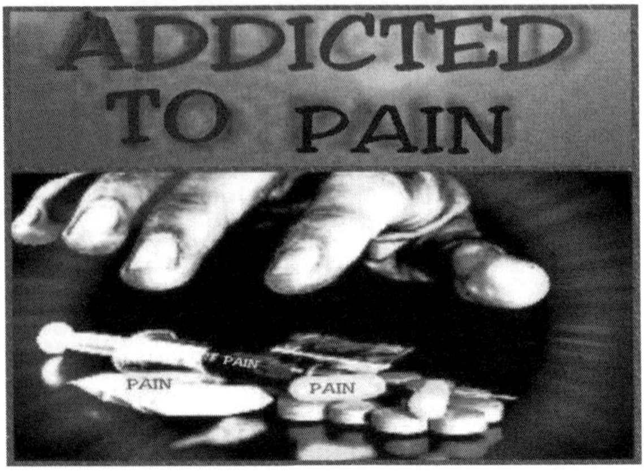

#

Addicted To Pain *#*

It seems like a great big conspiracy, against me, they keep on setting up.

But it doesn't matter how many times it occurs I still keep on getting up.

Over and over again continuously, steadfastly like a train, without letting up.

Even through all the heartaches and pain I endure I just can't get enough.

I have been hurt so many times and yet still I always keep on loving more.

Loving wrong, loving strong, sometimes uncertain and sometimes loving sure,

I always seem to attract the "wrong" kind of people to my inner sanctum.

Who only chooses to be with me and engage my emotions only to have some fun?

The kind of people that are pleasure seekers, who choose partners at random.

Having protected sex is safe, but my heart cannot be protected by a condom.

I must be fatally attracted to sorrow and take life for a game.

Is it that I keep on thinking love and infatuation are the same?

I always seek to find love in strange places where I have nothing to gain.

I must be hooked on heartache, and it seems, I'm addicted to pain.

I keep on living with the pain of rejection, whilst choosing not to accept the truth.

It seems there will be no rehabilitation from sorrow, pain is my "sweet tooth".

Immersed in denial I stay, embracing the anguish of another heart break, another day.

I'm a sucker for love, a hopeless romantic, why do I have to be this way.

Treating myself callously, with scant disregard for my heart, dangerous games I play.

Always seeming to love someone who sees me as dispensable, and they never stay.

I am like an archeologist searching for love in the pyramids of life, oh what an expedition.

Sometimes I feel like it's more like a militant extremist sent on a suicide mission.

My undying obsession, with love and finding my ''other half'' is like an emotional crucifixion.

I feel like I am dying a slow death inside because it seems like pain is my only addiction.

I must be fatally attracted to sorrow and take life for a game.

Is it that I keep on thinking love and infatuation are the same?

I always seek to find love in strange places I have nothing to gain.

I must be hooked on heartache, and it seems, I'm addicted to pain.

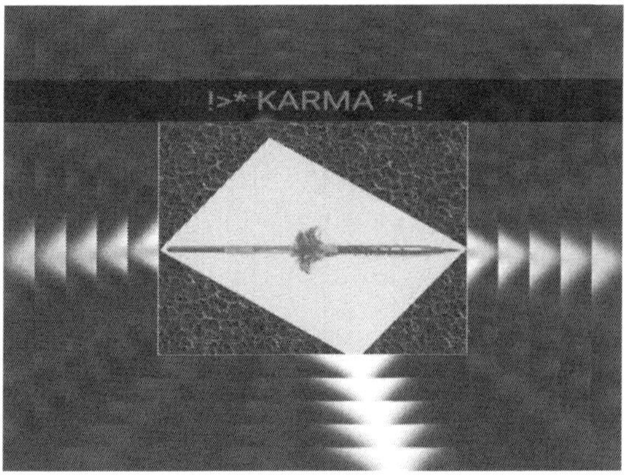

¥o ...KARMA... o¥

I am a product of very good karma...

From my many broken hearts I have learnt...

I have a way with words I'm a charmer...

I too have also been charmed and burnt...

A lot of people judge the book by the cover, without reading one page.

Experience teaches wisdom, but experience comes with age.

The longer you live the more you learn that's oh so very true.

You will be held accountable for all the bad things that you do.

I have broken many hearts and mine has been broken to pieces.

Balanced is the equation, but sometimes love feels fake like a prosthesis.

I try to put up a force field, trying to protect my heart with armor.

No matter how we run and try to hide, we can't escape from karma.

So now I have become…

I am a product of very good karma...

From my many broken hearts I have learnt...

I have a way with words I'm a charmer...

I have also been charmed and burnt...

Confuse not my easy-going personality for me being a fool.

I have learnt harsh lessons of life, I'm from the hard knock school.

These lessons cannot be learnt in a college or on a bar stool.

Experience teaches, "what you give is what you get" yeah that's the rule.

Now I have learnt to be cool and enjoy life, my demeanor is calmer.

I'm staying away from all the confusion, the gossiping and the drama.

Cultivating seeds of love and care, watering it and nurturing it like a farmer.

Fashioning my own destiny by my works, no longer worrying about karma.

My conscience is my guide…

I am a product of very good karma...

From my many broken hearts I have learnt...

I have a way with words I'm a charmer...

I have also been charmed and burnt…

o Finally *o*

A lot I have been through, all the stress and the headaches...

Crying at nights because of you, tears, enough to fill lakes...

Now I'm back to my old self, Deja Vu, now that I've gotten over you...

No more grief, I'm loving this feeling of relief, it's long overdue...

Finally!...

Finally, I'm no longer a slave to my emotions, not controlled by sorrow.

My sad yesterday has now been replaced by a happy optimistic tomorrow.

For a while I was buried in grief trying to get over you, needing a life to borrow.

From your cage my heart is free like a sparrow, pulled me back, now I fly like an arrow.

An enormous mountain of emotions inside of my heart, as high as the Himalayas.

I have now overcome and gotten immune to the games of all the "true playas".

I will no longer succumb to criticisms and be stereotyped by the naysayers.

I instead will hold myself in high regard amongst kings, queens and mayors.

Even though...

A lot I have been through, all the stress and the headaches...

Crying at nights because of you, tears, enough to fill lakes...

Now I'm back to my old self, Deja Vu, now that I've gotten over you...

No more grief, I'm loving this feeling of relief, it's long overdue...

After all the...

Scars from trauma, drama and emotional wars I wear them proudly like a badge.

The feelings of yearning and wanting to go back I try my best to dodge.

Feeling like I can't cope, wanting some rope or maybe a smoke or some scotch.

Sometimes when you lose love, move on and don't look back like the wife of Lot.

I was down and out, reminiscing about us and trying my best for us to get back.

My life was a mess, full of stress and unrest after our breakup's impact.

Now I've finally lost all feelings for you, I no longer have none honestly, in fact,

I'm feeling "alive", I've stopped yearning for you, luckily with my heart still intact.

Yet still...

A lot I have been through, all the stress and the headaches...

Crying at nights because of you, tears, enough to fill lakes...

Now I'm back to my old self, Deja Vu, now that I've gotten over you...

No more grief, I'm loving this feeling of relief, it's long overdue...

Finally!...

¥ Heartbreaks *¥*

Life is for living and sometimes you choose to share it.

Sometimes you crave that person to give your heart to for
them to care for it.

But then you may end up regretting you ever allowed them to
even get near it.

The one who you think is the best, sometimes causes you the
most distress.

Hearts are as fragile as glass, and once they are broken it
never mends.

Heartaches are devastating no matter how you try to make amends.

Love makes you open up your heart and it makes you vulnerable and naïve.

That doesn't mean you shouldn't love with all your heart again and believe.

Once you are hurt it's hard to get over it and be ready for a new start.

It's hard to love with a broken one so you may need a brand-new heart.

Loving with a broken heart is like trying to fly with broken wings.

Love and pain, it's not safe, but they both live on the same avenue and lane.

It's like running with a broken leg or driving a car on some broken rims.

No game, it's in the heart and brain and warms the soul like a burning flame.

Heartbreaks are like electricity, something you can't see but you can feel.

You just know it's there inside and you know that the feeling is real

It’s hard to overcome the pain but try to be strong, it will take time to heal.

Even when you know you might get hurt again you just can’t resist the appeal.

It’s so strange but things and time will change and rearrange with age.

The healing process is the first stage before you are ready to engage.

To write in the book of life your emotional love story on a new page.

Open up your heart and set free your innermost sensations from the cage.

It hurts a lot like broken limbs, it's unable to mend like other broken things.

But remember that falling in love is a gamble like when a token spins.

Loving with a broken heart is like trying to fly with broken wings.

¥ I Hate To Love *¥*

Sometimes I just hate to love.

But it's not that I love to hate.

It's because hate can't bring love.

But love can sometimes bring hate.

A broken heart always leaves me distressed.

Lost in my emotions and still searching for "me".

Trying to find out who or what is best.

Wondering with whom and where I should be.

Dreading the impending failure of my heart's next test.

Just yearning in earnest for my soul to be free.

To reside in a place where my mind is at rest.

I hate what this thing called "love" is doing to me.

Sometimes I just hate to love.

But it's not that I love to hate.

It's because hate can't bring love.

But love will sometimes bring hate.

I thought love would make me happy, it would be fun.

But it has only brought a dark cloud with showers of rain.

My life has no more bright sky, no more shining sun.

Oh the pain of another heartbreak is driving me insane.

Oh I wish it could all be over with, I wish it could all be done.

But it has a permanent stain that is stuck in my brain.

So now even the slightest trace of "like" I try my best to shun.

Been hurt so many times, so now, far from love I try to run.

Sometimes I just hate to love.

But it's not that I love to hate.

It's because hate can't bring love.

But love will sometimes bring hate.

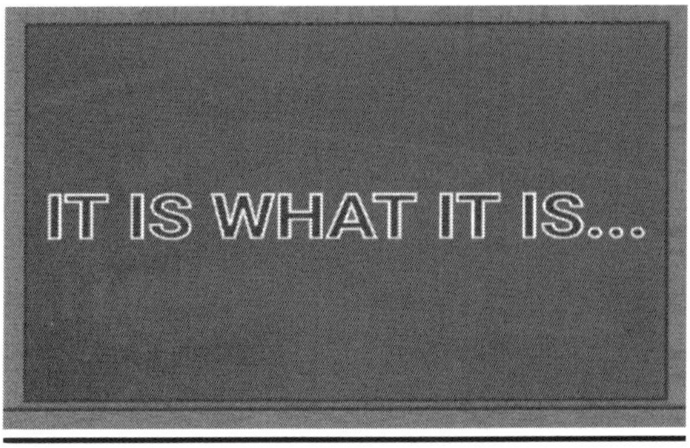

A It Is What It Is *A*

There are no guarantees in life that who you love will always love you the same.

You can give them the world and they will still play with your heart like a game.

People will do a lot of bad things to you and then still want to give you all the blame.

Excuses of all the things you were doing, though you never heard them yet complain.

It's so insane that you put them up so high on a pedestal and they left you in shame.

They didn't appreciate all that you did for them, sacrifices, and now it's all in vain.

Now you are left broken hearted, stressed, emotionally drained and living in pain.

Life goes on, pick up what remains, get it together and try to learn to love again.

Life is like this…

Such a shame that it really has to be like this, but it is what it is…

You endure all the pain and things remain the same, but it is what it is…

Life will sometimes make you but it will also break you, that's how life is…

We can only put our best foot forward and continue to live, it is what it is…

Being faithful and loving and caring to someone is no surety that they will remain true.

It is what it is no matter what you do, there are no guarantees that it will be reciprocated to you.

It is a blessing in life when you can find that special person, they are very far and very few.

I find it strange how bad things sometimes happen to good people who don't even have a clue.

Things can get messed up and what you did or what you are now to do, if only you knew.

Situations with no closure can leave you stuck like running on a treadmill, waiting in cue.

After all you've been through you still have to keep going, be strong and try to start over anew.

Your true love is still out there waiting on you, be patient even though it seems long overdue.

Life is like this…

Such a shame that it really has to be like this, but it is what it is…

You endure all the pain and things remain the same, but it is what it is…

Life will sometimes make you but it will also break you, that's how life is…

We can only put our best foot forward and continue to live, it is what it is…

★◆ Conflicting Feelings ◆★*

Life is a journey, while you are having fun and getting your groove on.

I'm watching with regret but it's all good though, I will accept it and move on.

I made my bed, filled with thorns, so now in it I surely will uncomfortably lie.

I'm a big boy, I live life without regrets, so therefore I won't make you see me cry.

I can live without you for sure, it's not like you are irreplaceable at all.

Even though you were always there for me, whether I fall or stand tall.

I live my life without fear and to be honest I don't really care.

Whether you stay or want to leave is neither here nor there.

But to be honest...

If only these words were true, that I say about you it would be so great...

It's fate, too late to speculate when you already closed your heart's gate...

There is no debate, I anticipate that date when myself I can emancipate...

I need to let go of these thoughts of us being intimate and try to elevate...

It's obvious that you have lost all interest in me but that's no big deal to me.

I am not even anxious or perturbed and it's clear for the whole world to see.

I never depend on other people to make me smile or to make me feel good.

If that was the case then maybe it would affect me a bit, yeah maybe it would.

The moments we shared are a thing of a very insignificant and distant past.

Though it seems like it was just the other day, I have gotten over you very fast.

Oh the mighty have fallen, you were once the love of my life and I was your hero.

I once had you on a pedestal, you were my everything but now I care zero.

But to be honest...

If only these words were true, that I say about you it would be so great...

It's fate, too late to speculate when you already closed your heart's gate...

There is no debate, I anticipate that date when myself I can emancipate...

I need to let go of these thoughts of us being intimate and try to elevate... Sigh...

A=+* Your Games *+=A

Continue doing what you're doing, I hope you're having fun.

I'm not intrigued by your games; I'll just watch the time run.

While the time runs, my feelings towards you will slowly expire.

Continue playing your games, I'll stand and watch like an umpire.

I will make a call and regulate the game every now and again.

But from being on your team or playing against you I will refrain.

I won't protest, I won't get angry and argue or even throw a tantrum.

I'll just let you have your fun until the game is over and your time is done.

I see you love to play games; love being sought after...

Wanting all my attention, simply warranting laughter...

Continue ignoring my feelings and enjoying your games...

Ultimately "we" will crash like a plane and burst into flames...

You seem to think the world revolves around you from floors to ceilings.

You want to have things your way all the time, disregarding my feelings.

I guess you don't realize that I too have a lot of needs and wants.

You treat me like I only need water, sun and oxygen like the plants.

Please don't think I'm "soft" because I speak with a lot of emotions.

My emotions transcend in seconds from a calm sea to raging oceans.

I'm really into you but it seems like I'm last on your "things to do list".

Ignoring my "needs" and "wants" can make my feelings cease to exist.

I see you love to play games; love being sought after...

Wanting all my attention, simply warranting laughter...

Continue ignoring my feelings and enjoying your games...

Ultimately "we" will crash like a plane and burst into flames...

Tumultuous Feelings

I fell asleep thinking of you and woke up to…

Harsh lessons learnt at the heart's expense.

Feelings extend from the past, making the next tense.

It makes sense, to look back and reminisce on ancient,

memories of what, how, where and why, all things adjacent.

Complacent behavior leading to ultimate displacement.

Matters not who's fault, only seeking a replacement.

Still not accepting what the look on your face meant.

Now the only thing remaining is the pillowcase scent.

Things are never perfect, up and down it goes...

Picture perfect is a myth and everyone knows...

You said I wasn't strong enough and you were right...

To the world I am superman but you are my kryptonite...

Reality started to soak in, as time passed by and days went.

Waiting for that call, time and place just state when.

For all the good that was done this is the repayment.

No it wasn't that? What are you trying to say then?

I'm lost in your words please rephrase your statement.

Oh, you felt like a victim of love, emotional enslavement.

I guess you already made up your mind to leave, it's too late then.

Go ahead and do your thing, have fun and party and go date men.

Just remember…

Things are never perfect up and down it goes...

Picture perfect is a myth and everyone knows...

You said I wasn't strong enough and you were right...

To the world I am superman but you are my kryptonite...

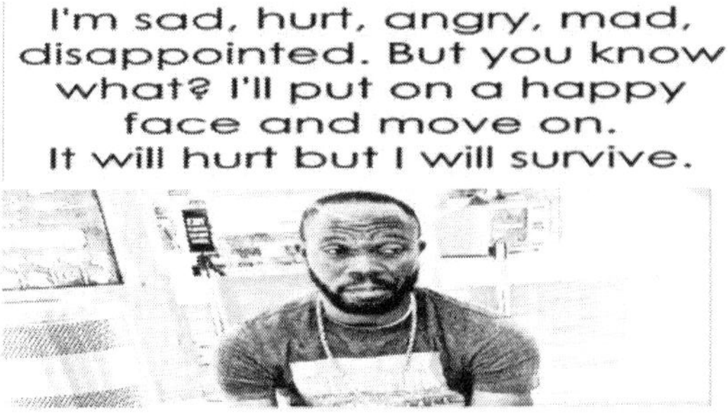

+ Happily Disappointed *+*

You kept saying you were going to leave and I kept saying no day.

You started to seem distant but I still didn't believe you, no way.

Even when you stopped calling, I just brushed it off with a smile.

I know that's how you are, knowing you, you will be back in a while.

Then you didn't answer my calls or reply to my texts, especially at night.

Thought you were going through a phase and would soon be alright.

When I found out you were "busy with him" I was going through shock.

I tried to get through to your heart but it seems you have changed the lock.

Just so you know...

I am happily disappointed that you found "that one"...

At first it was all good and cool, but now I am the sad one...

Played a game of "being the man", thinking you couldn't leave...

I now show a happy face with a heavy heart, living in disbelief…

I see you and your new life, becoming a wife, it's all good.

I am very happy for you, it's true, because I know I should.

I see you got someone new, who is "much better" than me.

Well, I am very happy for you now, but disappointed it isn't me.

I see that bright smile; happy face and I see your glowing skin.

I smile back sarcastically, but to be honest, disappointment lies within.

When I saw you with your shiny new ring, I said I was so happy for you.

I am glad that you found happiness, but if only my words were true.

I still love you…

I am happily disappointed that you found "that one"...

At first it was all good and cool, but now I am the sad one...

Played a game of "being the man", thinking you couldn't leave...

I now show a happy face with a heavy heart, living in disbelief...

¥ Caught Up *¥*

You see me going through my daily paces, encountering different faces from different races in different places.

You know not my struggle in this jungle called life, the war and the strife, it cuts like a knife, "betrayed" by my own wife.

Well, not really betrayed, because I "played" and "laid" even though I was afraid of the ultimate price I paid.

She is gone but I know she'll be back, if not, I hope she'll get back on track, story of my life, stability I lack, into my feelings hack.

I wish I could do a factory reset like a gadget then I bet I would get a fresh start, no sweat, that hasn't happened yet.

So still I await, for a date, to become my soul mate... knock at the gate… time for work, my drive is here, I'm late.

One day I may see you and...

If you ask how I'm doing I will say fine, it's not like you plan to help with these problems of mine...

It's not as if you plan to contribute a nickel or a dime, just being courteous, but please, not on my time…

Not at my expense, not when I'm still unstable and stability I'm here seeking to find…

I am just here by myself trying to find "me" while caught up in these thoughts in my mind…

I think the best thing was for her to go, because even though I knew about "Joe", my feelings continued to grow, so I kept it on the low.

Living in denial, like a guilty criminal on trial, without a lawyer to dial.

Thinking not of my own heart, just not wanting us to part, especially since my mom had warned me from the start, but I thought she was wrong, until I got caught.

Caught up in my feelings, now that everything is revealing, I lay looking up at the ceiling, my happiness you were stealing.

What's the meaning of a vow if now you allow another man to reap the seeds I sow?

But I'm no jerk so while you twerk, me and your friends...
(Buzzer sounds...) Time to get back to work.

One day you may call and...

If you ask how I'm doing I will say fine, it's not like you plan to help with these problems of mine...

It's not as if you plan to contribute a nickel or a dime, just being courteous, but please, not on my time…

Not at my expense, not when I'm still unstable and stability I'm here seeking to find…

I am just here by myself trying to find "me" while caught up in these thoughts in my mind…

*: * Thank You *:*

My Ex:

Thanks to you I have now lost my pride without getting you to be a bride...

Thanks to you I'm now ashamed of who I've become...

You tore my heart, I trusted you with everything...

Now all I can say is thanks to you, all I have is nothing...

I saw you as my number one hero but deep within you cared zero.

You cared zero about me and my stupid emotions but thanks to you.

Sigh, you made me confide in you, when you knew you weren't true.

I had no idea of how deceitful you were but hey thanks to you.

You spread your bed but you're not the one who lay in it, I did! Not you.

How could I be so foolish! But what can I say, huh, thanks to you?

I felt so comfortable in your arms, your smile fooled me, your charms.

Your voice, oh i don't want to hear it!!! But thanks to you for all the use, the abuse.

For all the hurt you put me through! Yeah, thanks to you!

Thanks to you I have become more mature...

Thanks to you things I used to do, I do them no more...

I'm sorry for all the pain I put you through...

I have learnt my lessons and it's all thanks to you...

I saw that you went through hell on earth, total meltdown.

You were stressed and depressed because of me and always felt down.

I didn't know that you felt so strongly about me, too blind to see.

With all the arguing and fighting between you and me, I needed to be free.

I was too immature to realize that it was love that caused you to act that way.

I was too caught up in being "the man" in the streets everyday wanting to "play".

Thanks to you I now changed my route and know what life is all about.

You made me become a much better man, I now understand, no doubt.

Thanks to you I see a new way, although the price of your happiness was a lot to pay...

Thanks to you....

+* Thoughts In My Head *+*

Here I sit in deep thought, of what, where, when and how.

Deep thoughts of me and you and the whole situation now.

Thoughts of why that happened, there, then, in that way.

Thinking about what we could have done to fix it on that day.

Pride is a poison chalice that leads to us being vindictive.

Fatal like tobacco to our lungs and yet still it is so addictive.

If only we had put love high and above petty stuff, no issue.

Our relationship wouldn't have been discarded like used old tissue.

These thoughts in my head hold me hostage to the past...

Times that we spent, memories melted like plastic, so fast...

A whirlwind of emotions, seeing your reflection in the glass...

Relationships built on the opinions of friends first, will never last...

Trying to move on but struggling with the thoughts of letting go.

Memories clouding my judgment, trying to get back, but getting no.

I don't handle rejection well, especially when I have been there.

These thoughts in my head, towards you, are loving and sincere.

It's like trying to walk, but you can no longer use your legs.

It's like these thoughts want me to fill round holes with square pegs.

I still remember that day when you came and caught her in my bed.

I lost you and I lost her; all I have left are the memories in my head.

These thoughts in my head hold me hostage to the past...

Times that we spent, memories melted like plastic, so fast...

A whirlwind of emotions, seeing your reflection in the glass...

Relationships built on the opinions of friends first, will never last...

! THINKING OF YOU *!*

As the rain cascades from the sky.

I sat by my window thinking about her, my one and only.

To contain these emotions so hard I try.

But the bittersweet memories are killing me slowly!

Her face was imprinted on my mirror. I blush at hearing her name.

All this love rushing through my heart...

Smiling for no reason like a person drove insane.

Wishing now I could stop them from the start.

All I wanted but didn't achieve flashes before my eyes..

Becoming extremely fearful of losing it forever..

My favorite hellos and most painful goodbyes..

The source from which I gained joy and pleasure...

Confused and broken, angry and betrayed..

Unhappy, sorrowful, hurt and frustrated..

The wounds left after all I felt got slayed..

My entire dreams had been manipulated..........

This has happened before, what we have been through....

As we sit here thinking of each other, you of me, me of you....

Simultaneously our hearts beat in cohesion and that's true....

Lost in time, thinking of you, lost in love, the feeling of Deja Vu....

I left without an explanation, a notation, no form of information.

Speculation, emotional dehydration, leaves a peculiar sensation.

Your erotic infiltration into my life led to intimidation.

Soul plane my means of transportation, emotional deportation.

In other words, I was so caught up in my emotions, mixed feelings.

Feelings revealing, had me kneeling, for you my heart appealing.

Appealing for you was the decision of my heart without my permission.

Therefore, Intermission was the only decision, liberation was the mission.

I had to be free from your spell that you cast upon my little heart.

It was love at first thought, like a fly in your web I was caught.

The feelings I developed were like no other, I had to leave.

Please believe, I didn't have any bad deeds up my sleeve.

No words could express the feelings you invoked within my soul.

My heart is my most treasured possession and it is what you stole.

I had to run, blame me not, I couldn't afford it, it's all I got.

I took my heart and ran, not looking back like the wife of Lot....

No pillar of salt... It's not your fault...

This happened before, what we have been through....

As we sit here thinking of each other, you of me, me of you....

Simultaneously our hearts beat in cohesion and that's true....

Lost in time, lost in love, the feeling of Deja Vu....

*A*HURTFUL * TRUTH *A*

Situations arise that sometimes require evasive action.

When sensitive questions are asked, lying is your first reaction.

It will be worse when you lie and the truth will be revealed later.

That is when the disappointment and hurt will be greater.

You may lie to avoid hurting my feelings whenever you lust.

One moment of joy is enough to destroy many years of trust.

It is never harder to speak the truth, please don't tell me you can't.

Life is full of temptations and a perfect relationship is not what I want.

Just....

Give me the truth, give it all no matter how harsh it may seem.

I would rather be disappointed than to be living in a "dream".

They say the truth is an offense but that's what I rather.

Hurt me with the truth, with the sweet lies don't bother.

Comforting lies are good for the moment, a temporary solution.

The truth is much more potent, no emotional pollution.

Relationships are built on the need for love and trust.

Most times it is destroyed by personal greed and lust.

Nobody is perfect so people will betray and deceive you.

However, consistent lying will make it very hard to believe you.

We all make mistakes sometimes, but it is how we treat it.

I don't want you to tell me lies and think it will delete it.

Just...

Give me the truth, give it all no matter how harsh it may seem.

I would rather be disappointed than to be living in a "dream".

They say the truth is an offense but that's what I rather.

Hurt me with the truth, with the sweet lies don't bother.

¥ Walking On Eggshells *¥*

Stepping gently, trying not to damage your feelings.

My weight is too much for this journey, exhaustion tells.

The only safe path I see is if like a spider I can walk in ceilings.

No matter how I try, feelings get damaged, like eggshells.

I can't help but walk this way, I didn't choose this path.

Love is something to treasure, and feelings are a token.

It is not my intention to hurt, so spare me please from your wrath.

I try my best, but I walk on eggshells, like glass feelings are broken.

I feel like I'm walking on eggshells, trying my best...

No matter how gently I step, they crack, I fail the test...

I'm walking on eggshells, that's the way you make me feel...

It's an impossible task, how can I avoid hurting you, please keep it real...

It's like there is nothing I can do or say to gain your approval.

Even the smallest of things without a minute to think.

You greet it with a negative vibe, instantaneous disapproval.

You take me to the brink, with this poison wine that we drink.

This wine we call "love" is damaging my heart a lot, times twenty.

When we just met everything was great, that was only for a while.

Then you became insecure and selfish and now I'm feeling empty.

No more joy, no more smile, oh this relationship is so fragile.

I feel like I'm walking on eggshells, trying my best...

No matter how gently I step, they crack, I fail the test...

I'm walking on eggshells, that's the way you make me feel...

It's an impossible task, how can I avoid hurting you, please keep it real...

* TIME *

Sometimes in life you are stressed and in despair.

At times things happen that you wish you could share.

Anytime things like these happen that causes sorrow.

You wish you could rewind to yesterday and skip to tomorrow.

At that moment in time your whole world comes to a halt.

Sitting and watching time, wondering why and whose fault.

Who did or didn't do what, is it your fault, theirs or mine?

One thing for sure, we can never turn back the hands of time.

The thing called time is the master of all things...

Hearts become victims of what time sometimes brings...

Time is also sometimes the key to your heart's healing...

Words can't always express what you're truly feeling...

Time is a great teacher and it is also a very cruel master.

In good times it moves fast but in bad times it's slow, never faster.

Good times seem to disappear and for them again you yearn.

Bad times are like the hardest lesson that takes forever to learn.

It's never something to take easy or to give little thought.

The pain it brings is like a terminal illness that rips your heart apart.

As time passes by you will have to deal with the pain you feel.

Just remember the passing of time is also the best medicine to heal.

This thing called time is the master of all things...

Hearts become victims of what time sometimes brings...

Time is also sometimes the key to your heart's healing...

Words can't always express what you're truly feeling...

It's funny how time somehow holds the key to your future.

As weird as it sounds it's a harsh judge but also a very good tutor.

Time oftentimes dictates what happens where and how to you.

You sit and think back while time passes, wondering what to do.

It controls your destiny, interestingly, even though it's never seen.

Sometimes I wonder if it's real, I wonder if you know what I mean.

The things that happen to you sometimes in life, it's like a crime.

There is nothing to do but to hold tight and ride the waves of time.

The thing called time is the master of all things...

Hearts become victims of what time sometimes brings...

Time is also sometimes the key to your heart's healing...

Words can't always express what you're truly feeling...

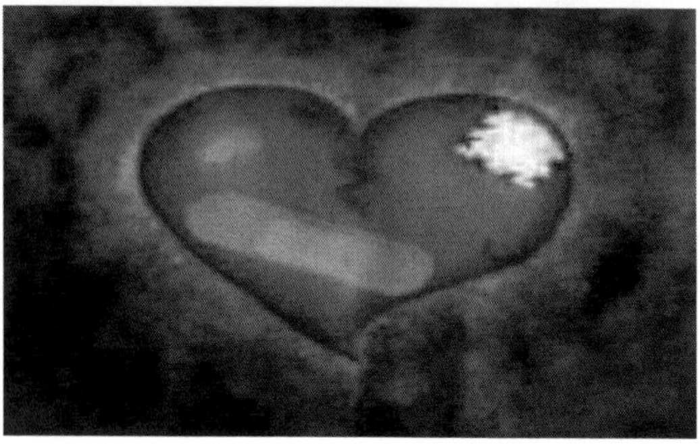

Chronicles Of A Broken Heart *#*

I gave you my all and everything and you still wanted more than I could ever give.

Love is such a blessing and a treasure and you got the best of my life that I had to live.

We were quite an item, everyone wanted to have a wonderful love like ours.

In the garden of my heart, you were undoubtedly the most beautiful of all flowers.

We were always together everywhere like birds of a feather and peas of a pod.

Right now, not having you in my life is the culmination of being miserable and sad.

I love you so dearly, love incarnate, physical and mental, the sweetest emotion.

Those smooth and silky, soft tender kisses, feathery touches making no commotion.

My love for you seems too good to be true like it was enhanced by a magic potion.

I know it's true love, pure like water from the spring so I discarded that silly notion.

You are a part of my every fiber, absorbed in every inch of my skin like lotion.

My love for you was not trivial or accidental, it flows like the river to meet the ocean.

There was a time when I would have done almost anything to have you around me.

Girl you were my beginning with no end, my lover, my heart, my girl and my friend.

Then all at once you changed drastically and my world came crashing down around me.

Since then, there have been no more happy moments, only loneliness surrounds me.

Anything your heart desired you would have gotten it as soon as you could think.

If it was required, I would have gotten water from the moon
for you to drink.

For you I would swim across the widest ocean and paint the
entire sky pink.

And then in the blink of an eye, like “The Titanic” our “Love
Boat” began to sink.

Was it something very bad that I did or was it something that
I should and did not?

Was it you being overzealous and materialistic and was this
relationship all a sinister plot?

I gave you my all, invested my time and my soul and heart
and nothing is all I got.

When you said it was over it was a shock, my body felt numb
like I just got shot.

You have now made my usually happy and bright life
become like the sky, ever so blue.

All the days of my life and the people I have come across
only you gave me something new.

Without you, I am nothing at all, you are my all and
everything and that’s oh so true.

If only you knew what I’ve been through, broken hearted, but
I am still in love with you.

There was a time when I would have done almost anything to
have you around me.

Girl you were my beginning with no end, my lover, my heart,
my girl and my friend.

Then all at once you changed drastically and my world came
crashing down around me.

Since then, there have been no more happy moments, only
loneliness surrounds me.

+ Rainy Days *+*

Sitting here looking through the window at the rain.

I'm wondering if my heart can overcome all the pain.

Do I wait for you, or do I move on and stay in my lane?

Sitting here I wonder if the sun will ever shine for me again.

My life is weathered and battered by all those dark rainy days.

I keep fighting to overcome but still I stay stuck in this rainy phase.

I hope it will soon change to brighter days with the passing of time.

Right now, I am still stuck in the mud of sorrow and it seems like a crime.

I am a victim and just a pawn of the game that a lot of heartless people play.

A beneficiary of the stress and depression associated with their evil ways.

I don't know what I could have done in my lifetime to be treated so unkind.

All I have are only deep thoughts of loving and caring harbored in my mind.

Sitting here looking through the window at the rain.

I'm wondering if my heart can overcome all the pain.

Do I wait for you, or do I move on and stay in my lane?

Sitting here I wonder if the sun will ever shine for me again.

I try my very best to hide my sorrow but I know the pain still shows.

I sit looking through life's window, waiting in earnest to see my rainbows.

Some people say I am weak, only those who feel it will ever get to know.

It's very depressing and stressful but that's just the way my rainy day goes.

I keep waiting in vain over and over again just to get your texts or your calls.

I'm drowning in my sorrow wanting to hear your voice again within these walls.

Sometimes I hear a sound and I swear it's your footsteps I hear in these halls.

Wishing it were true, but my sunshine has gone, and for me only the rain falls.

Sitting here looking through the window at the rain.

I'm wondering if my heart can overcome all the pain.

Do I wait for you, or do I move on and stay in my lane?

Sitting here I wonder if the sun will ever shine for me again.

¥ **Broken Wings** *¥*

Only time can be able to help heal these broken wings so we can fly again.

To once more reach the heights of ecstasy on cloud nine in the sky again.

To make you happy I have failed once but my best this time I will try again.

Please let me in your life once again and you will never have to cry again.

I know it's so very hard to forgive me but you know my love is not false.

I would love to say that I am very sorry for all the hurt that I have caused.

Please let us both try to put all the mishaps of the turbulent past on pause.

I felt like we both cheated the codes of love and then we broke all the laws.

We treated our love life like it was a game and that's why we gambled and lost.

I think it was due to the fact that we were young and naive and moving too fast.

Let us try to make bygones be bygones and let us please stop dwelling on the past.

Built on the proper foundation of trust through the test of time our love will last.

Only time can be able to help heal these broken wings so we can fly again.

To once more reach the heights of ecstasy on cloud nine in the sky again.

To make you happy I have failed once but my best this time I will try again.

Please let me in your life once again and you will never have to cry again.

Me without you is like a pilot on a plane in flight without hearing or sight.

Navigating a left turn that takes you nowhere at all, it's just not right.

I truly need you by my side and I won't ever stop or give up that fight.

Just the thought of losing your love gives me a sudden chill like frostbite.

I'm suffocating, I can't breathe whenever I try to live without your love.

If we were not meant to be, then why does your hand fit mine like a glove?

To have you in my life every night I pray beneath the moon and stars up above.

For time to heal my broken wings so I can fly once again in the sky like a dove.

Only time can be able to help heal these broken wings so we can fly again.

To once more reach the heights of ecstasy on cloud nine in the sky again.

To make you happy I have failed once but my best this time I will try again.

Please let me in your life once again and you will never have to cry again.

(:) Taboo Love *(:)*

To say I'm missing you, would be an understatement, no
words can express.

When I'm with you, or even just seeing you, there isn't
enough of you or excess.

Now you are apart, from my heart, but still in my every
thought, my next best.

Drowning in misery, plotting in theory, conspiring mentally,
for me no less stress.

Come back to me, I know you want to, but only because of
your family and friends.

They never liked me to begin, they just tolerated our union as
a means to an end.

If I wasn't smart, they would have used me and refused me,
all they do is pretend.

They care not about your wellbeing, they only care about
what I have to spend.

They say love is very blind, but our kind is heart, soul and
mind, our love is forever true.

If only they knew the things, we've been through they
wouldn't try to separate me and you.

Chances to find a love like this are few, so from my point of
view, for you, anything I'd do.

What we share, none compare, I'll always be here, even
though us being together is taboo.

Listen not to their negative talk, when they give advice, they
mean you no good.

They care not for you, to sell you the highest bidder, they
sure would if they could.

They influence you to leave me, not for better but only to get
me out of the picture.

It's not about someone to love you more, or for your
happiness just for someone richer.

Trying to manipulate you to fulfill their needs, but our need
for each other is greater.

I try to move on, get my groove on, but to my body and mind
my heart is like a traitor.

It refuses to let go of the past and let the past lie, it beats only
for you despite how I try.

No matter what they do, though it's taboo, I can't give up on
you and I don't know why.

They say love is very blind, but our kind is heart, soul and
mind, our love is forever true.

If only they knew the things we've been through they
wouldn't try to separate me and you.

Chances to find a love like this are few, so from my point of
view, for you, anything I'd do.

What we share, none compare, I'll always be here, even
though us being together is taboo.

*^> Mirage <^*

Right now, I'm here sitting…

I am sitting here with an empty glass in my hand, pretending to be drinking.

In my mind it's like a beehive, not sweet, but buzzing with the things I'm here thinking.

Thinking about you and me, the way we were and how we are now, the actions of time.

How good we were together and how we are now, how things have changed, such a crime.

I was loving the vibe you always would bring, but to you it was nothing, just another fling.

Another conquest, another victim to be seduced, you are poisonous like a scorpion's sting.

I was warned that you were a rolling stone gathering no moss as you infinitely rolled along.

I went along and enjoyed the ride because I knew to other people our hearts belong.

We are not bound together nor are we carved in stone...

You have your husband and I have my lovely wife at home...

We had a moment and you had enough and decided to move...

I won't lie to myself as much as I liked you, there is nothing to prove...

The truth is I really cared for you and I'm only human and I have feelings too.

You played your game well from the beginning, but I saw right through you.

Feelings were there but still it was cool, sometimes it's fun to just play along.

I have been around these streets long enough so I can walk away and be strong.

I really enjoyed it all and you're a really fun person, cool to hang out with, I like that.

I know all good things must come to an end so there's no need for me to fight that.

It's a bit premature though but that's cool, do your thing, I know it was premeditation

There was no dedication, some seduction, but no broken heart needing medication.

That's for sure…

We are not bound together nor are we carved in stone...

You have your husband and I have my lovely wife at home...

We had a moment and you had enough and decided to move...

I won't lie to myself as much as I liked you, there is nothing to prove...

Depression

With so much on my mind and I don't even know what I'm thinking about or where to begin it's like standing at the highway and seeing the cars passing so fast it's just one big blur.

When you are a tower of strength for everyone to lean on and you become overwhelmed not knowing where to lean or who to call, wanting to be strong, afraid to fall.

Depression is real and it comes when you least expect it, you just open your eyes and it's staring you right in the face, you don't know what triggered it or how it came to fruition.

You know not what to do or say, things in your mind that won't come out, wanting to scream, wanting to shout, opening your mouth and the words just won't come out..

Trying to say what you feel but you don't even know if it is real, so you try your best to conceal, clasp your hands and you kneel, opening up your heart making an appeal.

You feel a heavy burden is on you, like you are walking with the expectations of the world on your shoulders, sack of rocks, heavy boulders, still you push on just like a soldier.

Depression is real and only who feels it knows…

It's something that's hard to deal with and it hardly shows…

It doesn't prejudice where, when, what or even who…

Beyond that smiling face nobody knows what you're going through…

Family, friends and coworkers look up to you for strength and to be a comforting shoulder, but sometimes you need a shoulder too, you have to be strong.

Sometimes you need to feel weak, to be comforted, to be taught and reassured, you want to get that emotional support so your heart can be poured..

But nobody knows this and you can't expose your weakness because it's "not who you are".

You are supposed to always be strong for everybody who looks up to you.

Always be the fortress of strength and comfort, but as the saying goes "who is going to watch for the watchman", "who is going to secure the security".

It's real and it's a sign of weakness so nobody wants to admit it.

Everybody deals with it in their own way, some drink, smoke, sniff, inject or swallow.

Some slash, tie a rope and jump or use a gun, sometimes all you need is a hug and a voice to say “it's going to be ok” when it's all said and done.

Depression is real and only who feels it knows…

It's something that's hard to deal with and it hardly shows…

It doesn't prejudice where, when, what or even who…

Beyond that smiling face nobody knows what you're going through…

It's not easy when you spend your life solving everybody else's problems with them not knowing you have a lot of serious problems of your own.

Then the pressure builds up and you don't know how to release it.

Especially when you are used to being strong and not accustomed to feeling weakness.

It's a challenge to deal with “the unknown”, and most times you just need a shoulder to cry on, to let it all out.

That feeling of stress leaving your body it's like that burp that eases your indigestion, that moment you start to feel like yourself again.

It's not an easy thing to overcome, sometimes you just want to sit in silence with someone not saying a word, just holding hands and enjoying the aura of golden silence.

Looking at the stars at night while listening to the sound of water rushing into the shore.

Inner peace is one of life's greatest gifts that we should cherish and adore.

Depression is real and only who feels it knows…

It's something that's hard to deal with and it hardly shows…

It doesn't prejudice where, when, what or even who…

Beyond that smiling face nobody knows what you're going through…

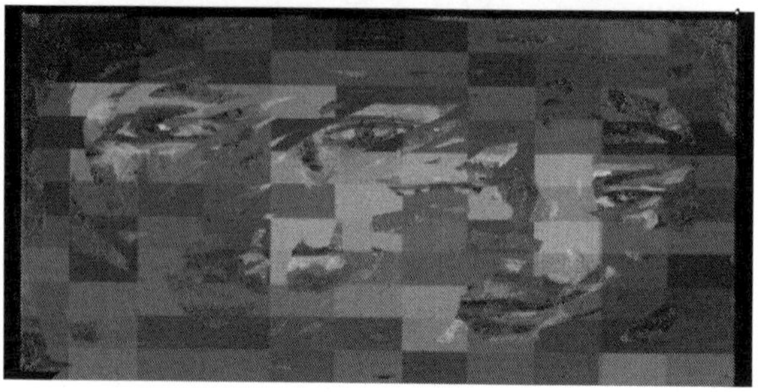

*! *@!* Hallucinations *!@*!*

I keep on seeing you walking on the street but I can't ever seem to catch up to you, like an illusion.

I don't know if it is deja vu but it's a lot of confusion, all I know is that I need some form of resolution.

I am losing my mind, the constant thoughts of us and how we were, needs to come to a conclusion.

It is further aided and abetted by my self-imposed seclusion, no intrusion not accepting contribution.

Going to the beach at night by myself and drinking liquor and trying my best to drown all my sorrows.

They seem to be very good swimmers because they will always reappear again first thing tomorrow.

It seems like this life of mine is not working out too well, I think I may need a different one to borrow.

Still, I continue along the same trajectory, towards my destination of pain, the target for this lonely arrow.

My mind is very unstable and it is as confused as it can be…

Trying my best to stay focused but it keeps playing tricks on me…

Everyday knowing I can't afford to break I've got to stay strong…

Then along comes another round of these hallucinations..

I try my best to overcome the test of my mental state which is so frail but I always seem to fail.

Even when I do my utmost best to pay attention to every small detail and paper trail it's still no avail.

I still keep on thinking of you obsessively and all my futile attempts at resistance get derailed.

The worst thing about it all is that I enjoy being locked in thoughts of you, refusing to be bailed.

Mental penetration is such a sweet sensation, only if our coordination was a balanced equation.

Concentration on the situation, exaggeration of relations devoid of conversation, all in my imagination.

Celebration for elevation from isolation, no medication for the duration of dedication of my frustration.

No reservation about the complication, lost in contemplation
if it is real or illumination of hallucination.

My mind is very unstable and it is as confused as it can be…

Trying my best to stay focused but it keeps playing tricks on
me…

Everyday knowing I can't afford to break I've got to stay
strong…

Then along comes another round of these hallucinations..

Sweet Lies *#*

They say lying lips are an abomination.

But sweet words lead to infatuation.

Words can paint a picture for the blind.

Feelings that were lost, these words can find.

Right words at the right time can soothe the soul.

Even when stress and strains take a toll.

Comforting words are music to the ears.

Drying tears from faces and removing fears.

Sweet words killing ever so softly, silent cries.

Saying what you want to hear despite all the tries.

Listening attentively between deep sighs.

Trying your best not to fall victim to sweet lies.

Saying what you want to hear and not the way it is.

Truth when spoken hurts, so sweet lies persist.

Words to make you better the soul it will soothe.

When you are having a rough time, they will smooth.

What sounds good sometimes is better than truth.

It can give sight to the blind and give the old some youth.

Even when you think all is lost and you accept defeat.

Problems can easily be solved with a lie so sweet.

Sweet words killing ever so softly, silent cries.

Saying what you want to hear despite all the tries.

Listening attentively between deep sighs.

Trying your best not to fall victim to sweet lies.

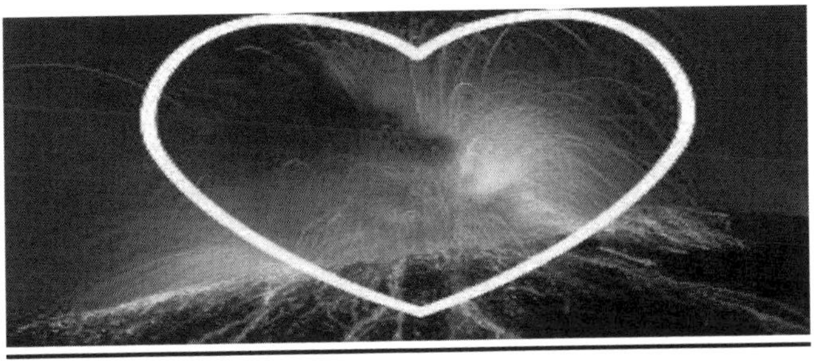

*: * Emotional Eruptions *: *

I used to feel so intimidated by my love for you that I would always compromise to "make it work".

It's as if I forgot I had a life and a voice too.

I cared so much about you that I forgot to care about me.

Now is the time, from you I am gonna break free.

Break free from your walls and fences that you use to keep me in captivity.

A captive of an emotional prison, I'm a victim of your insecurity.

From you I have got to break free...

I deserve better than this...

It's time to think about only me...

This time I won't look back, I promise...

Every time I leave, I have this itching feeling like a rash.

This feeling to come back, but when I do you put me in a fixed deposit like cash,

Right now, I unleash my emotional eruptions, it happens in a flash.

Feelings flow like lava whatsoever it touches burns to ash.

No longer a prisoner, I saw that loophole and made a dash.

Feelings flow free like water in the sea and make a great splash.

Tears like a tsunami, washing away my sorrows as they crash.

That's how I did it...I did it for me...

I went beyond my limits...

I had to set myself free...

And now…

I reclaim my heart, it's no longer for rent or lease.

Now you choose to show you care, now you realize how much you love me, oh please.

You never know what you have till it's gone away.

I gave it all to you and you threw it all away.

You used to make me feel like for you I was never good enough.

Now it's over, prepare to get burnt as my emotions erupt.

I'm burning my bridges and renouncing rights of passage.

Cutting all strings attached and getting rid of excess baggage.

= Footsteps In The Hallway *=*

I used to think of you for just a while...

But now, I think of you all day...

Sometimes I just sit and smile...

When I hear footsteps in the hallway...

Faint echoes, emotional remnants, are all that remains.

Distant memories keep coming back, the joys and the pains.

Constantly I think of what could have happened or could have been.

Just when I think I'm over you, it’s when the flashbacks begin.

The smell of your perfume lingers, although it's a bit faint.

Your presence is still here on these lonely walls like paint.

Waiting to hear your voice, patiently waiting for your calls.

All that remains are your footsteps lingering in these halls.

I used to think of you for just a while...

But now, I think of you all day...

Sometimes I just sit and smile...

When I hear footsteps in the hallway...

It may not be the most ideal situation, not what I would choose.

I always strive to win but sometimes in life you may lose.

Without you, this house is such a very different place.

Forever in my heart but still I long to see your face.

If I could see your smile or that look in your eyes, if only.

If I could have you once again, my life wouldn't be so lonely.

Happy memories of us in my mind and heart are plenty.

Now that you are gone and left me, my life has become empty.

CHRONICLES OF A BROKEN HEART

I used to think of you for just a while...

But now, I think of you all day...

Sometimes I just sit and smile...

When I hear footsteps in the hallway...

A Different *A*

"What if it was all just different in your head"

"What if I was different instead"

My feelings I have for you are of a different sort.

It's from a different place, coming from a different part.

I think of you in a different way, a different thought.

Wishing you could love me if only you had a different heart.

If only we could want the same, instead of a different plan.

It would change my life and make me a very different man.

We both are the same even though we sing a different song.

We both have different feelings but they both are strong.

In life opposites attract no matter how different we are.

We both can still love each other no matter how far.

Distance may separate us but it can't keep us apart.

That distance is nothing when you're still in my heart.

I keep thinking about what could have happened, where and when.

What if I had made my move when I had the chance way back then.

Would you have changed your mind and seen me in a different way?

How much difference would it make if you heard the different things I had to say.

If you had given me a chance, I would have made a difference in your life.

It would all be different by now, I would have made you, my wife.

You may wonder if this poem is about a lie or if it's really true.

No need to think about anything different, it's really about you.

In life opposites attract no matter how different we are.

We both can still love each other no matter how far.

Distance may separate us but it can't keep us apart.

That distance is nothing when you're still in my heart.

¥ Relationship Blues **¥

Relationship blues...

It's nothing that's new…

It's not the thing we would choose...

Sometimes in life you gamble and lose...

You give your all and in return you only get abuse...

Relationship blues...

Sometimes it's going all smooth,

then something happens without an excuse…

You snap and it's like you just lost a fuse...

That's why we see so many crazy things on the news...

Relationship blues...

I've had my share; I've paid my dues...

Been there, done that, gotten applause and boos...

Had good, had bad, some smart, some with different views…

Some wild like a jungle lion or tame like the ones in the zoos...

Relationship blues…

It can take your life on many avenues…

From chilling on the corners with the crews…

To drown your sorrow in cigarettes and booze…

Appleton, rum, orange juice and gray goose…

Relationship blues…

Can drive you crazy, send your brain on a cruise…

Walking around dirty without wearing clothes or no shoes…

Even in the rubbish bin find yourself taking a snooze…

Jump from a building around your neck put a noose…

Relationship blues...

Some take it for a joke, some are not amused...

Sometimes the one you choose to give your heart refused...

Then it's like a bomb ticking that can't be defused...

BOOM!!!! Then all you're left with.....

Are relationship blues....

(Never Let You Go *) *

We have been through a lot of ups and downs.

With smiles I have filled your cups and with frowns.

You have been there for me when I needed you most.

Even when I acted like you were invisible like a ghost.

I know you love me a lot and want to be my only girl.

I may not say it out loud but to me you mean the world.

No longer do you have to wonder, now you know.

I will fall to temptation, but I will never let you go.

Never let go of my hand...

And I will do the same...

It may be hard to understand...

I know you think it is a game...

I never meant to play you for a fool.

It's just that at times my hormones will overrule.

Just know that no matter where I go or who I am with,

you are my heart and soul, promise me that you will never quit.

Temptations abound and I try but still eventually succumb to them.

Then I leave feeling guilty and promise myself that I won't do it again.

I gamble against the odds and become a victim of losses and wins.

I want us to get back to how we were, I miss seeing those grins.

Never let go of my hand...

And I will do the same...

It may be hard to understand...

I know you think it is a game...

A Now That You Are Gone *A*

Now that you are gone my life will never be the same.

It's like the end of a movie or the last play of a game.

Even though I played with your emotions, I cared a lot.

You gave me your all and in return, hurt is all you got.

I never really meant to cause you any hurt or any pain.

Such a waste for all these years to go down the drain.

Give my love another try, give me one more chance.

We have chemistry and rhythm, give me one last dance.

Even though.....

I can't stand this pain, I'm so numb, I can't walk…

If I even hear your name is like I'm dumb, I can't talk…

I am feeling helpless like a baby that has just been born...

I am nothing at all ever since you've been gone…

Now that you are gone, it seems nothing at all I am.

Kisses and hugs, moments that took my breath away, damn!

Now that you are gone from me, my life is now like a blank page.

We have grown stronger together and like fine wine, finer with age.

You took my life away from me, committed murder in the first degree.

Squeezed the air from my lungs, watched as I fell like a leaf from a tree.

You were the love of my life and to me you meant everything.

Without you in my life it isn't worth anything.

And now.....

I can't stand this pain, I'm so numb, I can't walk…

If I even hear your name is like I'm dumb, I can't talk…

I am feeling helpless like a baby that has just been born...

I am nothing at all ever since you've been gone…

I I'm Missing YOU *I*

I passed by your house today a couple minutes after four.

I was about to call out your name as I always did before.

That was when I remembered you're not around anymore.

I broke down and cried till my eyes were sore.

I'm missing YOU…

The other day I had a problem and thought it would be nice,

if I could call you to just hear your voice and ask for your advice.

But you weren't there and it's like sometimes I still can't realize.

What happened was a very unpleasant surprise.

I'm missing YOU…

Sometimes I still smell your scent in the air.

Someone speaks and I swear it's your voice I hear.

I know you are no longer here with me and it's clear.

Physically gone, but spiritually I know you are still there.

I'm missing YOU…

The other day I was just there sitting on my wall.

I was about to go with my friends to the mall.

I thought about you and was going to give you a call.

Then I remembered you weren't there after all.

I'm missing YOU...

Sometimes I get depressed whenever I hear your favorite song.

It hurts because you are gone and this is where you belong.

I see your picture and I can't help it but I try to be strong.

I know one day I will see you again and I am not wrong.

I'm missing YOU...

Memories

Sometimes my eyes get jealous of my heart…

You remain close to my heart but from my eyes you're far apart…

My heart can feel your love but my eyes can't see your face...

All I have are memories of you and me in time and space....

The moments we shared will forever be in my heart.

We gave it our all, though we knew it wasn't perfect from the start.

Our love hit the bull's eye, the center of the target like a dart.

It mesmerizes my whole being, of my life you will forever be a part.

I know that this feeling is like Victoria, but no secret, it's mutual.

Every day, what can I say, but stay this way, loving you as usual.

It seems like distance and time have become our greatest enemies.

All we have to share are just those treasured moments, memories.

Sometimes my eyes get jealous of my heart…

You remain close to my heart but from my eyes you're far apart…

My heart can feel your love but my eyes can't see your face...

All I have are memories of you and me in time and space....

There is the feeling that I let you go too easily; my emotions are at war.

Played like I was tough and now my heart is left with an emotional scar.

You are my love, my life, my woman, my wife, my sky, moon and my star.

You are close to my heart even though to my eyes you may be so far.

I need to see you again, I can only reminisce on the things we used to do.

I never meant to hurt your feelings, I never meant to break your heart in two.

I would give up the world if you should, promise that we could, start anew.

As long as I live I will always love you and I will never be able to forget you.

Sometimes my eyes get jealous of my heart…

You remain close to my heart but from my eyes you're far apart…

My heart can feel your love but my eyes can't see your face...

All I have are memories of you and me in time and space....

*! * Moment Of truth *! *

This is not just a poem.

It's the story of my youth

It is as real as it gets.

This is a moment of truth.

I think I'm gonna be old and lonely with no one to call my own.

I think I will have no one to turn to when I am depressed and feeling down.

The worst part is that it will be all my fault.

There is no one for me to blame but myself, my heart has been hardened like asphalt.

CHRONICLES OF A BROKEN HEART

I never allow anyone to get too close to me because I feel they are in pretense.

As soon as I feel they are getting too close to my heart I push them away and put up my defense.

This is not just a poem.

It's the story of my youth.

It is as real as it gets.

This is a moment of truth.

I guess that's what happens when you experience heartbreaks and pain.

It can be depressing although it doesn't stop you from loving again.

It makes you uncertain though and gives you second thoughts all the time.

It hurts and leaves you with emotional scars that may not be healed by time.

I don't know how, when, or whom, will break me free from this spell.

I hope I will find that little spark to set me free, but only time will tell.

This is not just a poem.

It's the story of my youth.

It is as real as it gets.

This is a moment of truth.

It is not a case of me not being able to love someone once more.

I just have problems trusting that person's motives, I'm so unsure.

I don't want to get hurt when I am giving my all.

I guess I'm just afraid it will hurt the next time I fall.

I still care and I am also still capable of showing you that love.

I just need someone to unlock the chains on my heart and set me free like a dove.

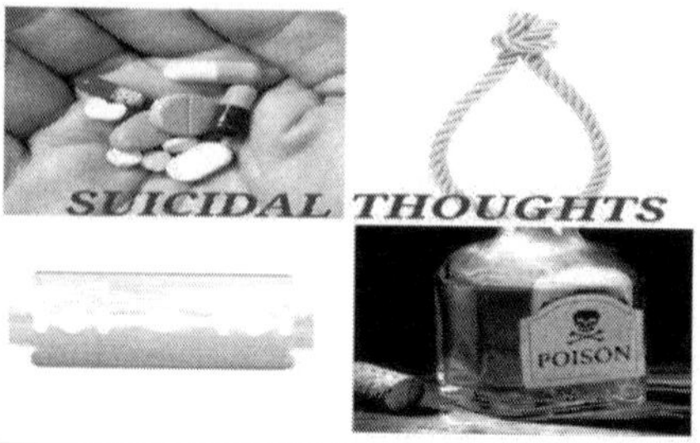

+ Suicidal Thoughts*+*

Pills and potions, ropes and razors, jumping from a twelve-storey building with no wings…

These thrills and emotions, hopes and saviors, pumping a life story within, filled with flings…

Hills and oceans, slopes and craters, dumping the trash inventory bin and filming the kings…

It's all just a lot of rhyming words with no real meaning, just like my life, on the edge leaning…

My life is on the brink of extinction, drinking and smoking and depression is my characteristic distinction.

I'm empty and drained, emotional eviction, numb and dumb not knowing how to overcome addiction.

I'm addicted to sorrows, drowning in self loathe and low self-esteem, with a lack of any real conviction.

I'm not wanted or loved, not worth the chance to become
someone's soulmate, emotional crucifixion.

Now it's time to end this suffering, time to bring this sad
story to an end, goodbye world, the end of me.

Nobody will miss me, they won't even notice that I'm gone,
until someone finds me hanging from a tree.

Then everybody will "love me" and will want me to rest in
peace, if only inside my mind they could see.

A whirlwind of thoughts, wondering why I can't find
happiness or success, I guess, it wasn't meant to be.

Pills and potions, ropes and razors, jumping from a twelve-
storey building with no wings…

These thrills and emotions, hopes and saviors, pumping a life
story within, filled with flings...

Hills and oceans, slopes and craters, dumping the trash
inventory bin and filming the kings…

It's all just a lot of rhyming words with no real meaning, just
like my life, on the edge leaning...

Oxygen! I can't breathe, I'm in need, so cold, suffocated by
expectations as my heart continues to bleed.

Can't fit in, only torturing my soul, trying to put a square peg in a round hole is not the challenge I need.

Negative thoughts are the water to life's stress, while planting suicidal thoughts in my mind like a seed.

I already got all the tools that I need to complete my evil deed about to proceed full speed and succeed.

I'm in a dark place, I can't see no escape exit, but I'm still holding the faith and pushing on to my credit.

Thinking twice, self-preservation is first on my list despite the urge to do it I won't submit, no merit.

I have got to be strong and not give in to the pressures of life and all this emotional stress I inherit.

No matter how bad it may seem there is always light at the end of the tunnel, hold on to your dream.

Never let go…

Pills and potions, ropes and razors, jumping from a twelve-storey building with no wings…

These thrills and emotions, hopes and saviors, pumping a life story within, filled with flings...

Hills and oceans, slopes and craters, dumping the trash inventory bin and filming the kings…

It's all just a lot of rhyming words with no real meaning, just like my life, on the edge leaning...

+ Move On *+*

Sometimes in life you will lose special people.

That one, the ones you think you need the most.

Maybe you have to cut them off because of hurt.

They may choose to leave you, or they may die.

But...

Let go, if you really care for them so much.

Let go, if they are not there for you to touch.

If they leave it's bad, if they die the situation worsens.

They may leave a haunting feeling like a ghost.

To know you are still here but they are under the earth.

Endlessly for them your heart will continue to cry.

Let go, move on and stop wondering why.
Let go, pay your dues with the tears in your eye.

People who hurt and then leave give the worst pain.
Especially when you never know what you did.
It often leaves you feeling useless or incomplete.
It leaves you feeling bitter and praying for karma.

Let go, they don't deserve to have someone like you.
Let go, it is obvious by the stupid things they do.

That person who you think you can't live without.
Your one and only may be the reason you are so lonely.
The person you give your heart to, breaks it in two.
They have nothing but pain to give, move on and "live".

Let go, love yourself first and others will too.
Let go, love you and to yourself please be true.

Trapped In Love *#*

The more time I spend here the more my heart turns to stone.

Among a very big population of people, but yet still I am all alone.

Wishing I could go for a walk, the streets I would love to roam.

Until that day of freedom, I'll close my eyes and picture home.

I am tired of looking at these barbaric scenes, tired of these walls and these bars.

I am tired of the daily and nightly routines of fighting physical, emotional and mental wars.

It leaves me traumatized and distressed and emotionally wounded with mental scars.

I would rather be on the beach or clubbing well dressed and driving rental cars.

Ever so often I sit and reminisce, thinking back on my life's happiness with utter regret.

Things changed in the blink of an eye and now I am being treated like nothing but a reject.

It seems like the scene from a movie, oh I wish I could fast forward it, rewind or eject.

This is what happens when your responsibilities to yourself you choose to neglect.

The more time I spend here the more my heart turns to stone.

Among a very big population of people, but yet still I am all alone.

Wishing I could go for a walk, the streets I would love to roam.

Until that day of freedom, I'll close my eyes and picture home.

There are a lot of things inside that keep me fighting with myself although you can't see.

I am succeeding to be whom and what social standards require of us but I am failing to be me.

So desperate am I to gain liberation I try to conform and try to be what they want me to be.

Little do they know that I am still the same, unchanged if not worse, only wanting to be free.

I am trapped in my own emotions, lost, and looking for a way out, myself I am trying to find.

Is it because I am a prisoner of someone else's heart, is that why I am being treated so unkind?

I hope I can be rehabilitated with the passing of time, but for now freedom is the only thing on my mind

I am an inmate, incarcerated in love, wanting to unwind, now I know why they say love is blind.

The more time I spend here the more my heart turns to stone.

Among a very big population of people, but yet still I am all alone.

Wishing I could go for a walk, the streets I would love to roam.

Until that day of freedom, I'll close my eyes and picture home.

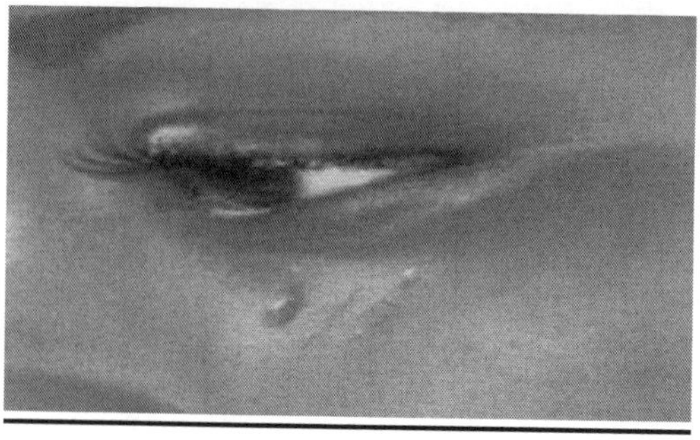

"*I*" Muted Tears "*I*"

Silently my heart weeps, it weeps not for the passing of a loved one.

It weeps and tries in vain to speak, trying to speak words of comfort.

I can't believe that after all we have been through, just like that, you are gone.

You came into my life and made me feel renewed just like a newborn.

I was lost and I was clueless to what true love really was.

Now thanks to you I can go on a hike and tell the world what it is like.

I try to fight this tension building up inside and repent.

I cry, my heart cries, my tears make no sound, my cries are silent.

It hurts to know that you're really gone away.

I know I'll be alright though without those fears.

Fears of hurting you with the things that I may say.

My eyes are dry but my heart cries muted tears.

These are a testament of my love for you, tears that I cry.

So miniature, that they cannot be seen by the naked eye.

At night when I try to sleep, they don't stain my sleeping pillow.

Like the wind that moves branches, the sound of the weeping willow.

Tears of sorrow I cry and tears of so much unwanted pain.

Tears of blood that flow through my veins, I hope I never cry again.

Life is a great big mystery and it's such a beauty to behold.

More than diamonds or gold is the story of true love as it begins to unfold.

Without you to hold I cry muted tears so bold, and my heart gets so cold.

Because....

It hurts to know that you're really gone away.

I know I'll be alright though without those fears.

Fears of hurting you with the things that I may say.

My eyes are dry but my heart cries muted tears.

(Alone In Despair *) *

I saw her the other day with her new man.

They both seemed so happy together as one.

As they held hands and crossed the street.

I prayed that they would get hit by a van.

I know my thoughts might seem to be evil.

But she left me when I needed her the most.

When the tax collectors seized my home and vehicle.

She disappeared in thin air like a ghost.

She left me all alone, down and in despair.

CHRONICLES OF A BROKEN HEART

I loved her so much but she didn't even care.

I tried to take care of her to the best of my ability.

She said love doesn't count only financial stability.

It's so unfair, I'm still hurting while she smiles.

To give her the best I would have walked a thousand miles.

Oh, where has her love gone so damn quickly?

She left me for another man oh so swiftly.

You know who's real when your back's against the wall.

I only hope and pray I am there to see her fall.

Then again, I won't render evil for evil, time will tell.

Until then, I wish your ass well and hope you burn in hell!!!

She left me all alone, down and in despair.

I loved her so much but she didn't even care.

I tried to take care of her to the best of my ability.

She said love doesn't count only financial stability

★÷★ That Awkward Moment ★÷★

You used to think you were their all and everything.

Flirt, date, indulge, relationship, engagement and wedding ring.

Now and forever, birds of a feather, genuine like leather.

Through the snowstorms, the sunshine and the rainy weather.

Then comes...

That awkward moment...

When you realize you aren't so smart.

That moment when you find out you were played.

Someone cheated and broke your heart.

When you thought they would have stayed.

That feeling of comfort and caring to your world they bring.

Then suddenly heartbreak gives you a mortal sting.

Your whole world comes abruptly crashing down on you.

You break, no more you can't take, a river of sorrows and tears fill a lake.

But then comes that awkward moment…

When you think you are the best, on top of the game.

That moment when you actually realize you are not.

It was all a figment of your imagination, all in the brain.

Sometimes the scenario is reversed and the situation is flipped.

Your life is like a movie and you write your own script.

Then you realize it wasn't a secret all along, they knew.

About the games you have been playing and the things you do.

Then you endure...

That awkward moment...

When you realize you aren't as tough as you thought.

That moment when you reach your breaking point.

Become a victim to all those emotional wars you fought.

Then you reminisce on “that awkward moment"...

«o Rain Again o»

I remember that day like it was just yesterday.

I made the worst mistake of my life when I walked away.

Walked away without looking back, not because of what you did.

But because of what I might do, my true feelings I hid.

Now suddenly once again out of nowhere here comes the rain.

Once more giving me the blues, those memories bring me pain.

To my heart it's like a strain, permanently like a stain.

Missing you, but in my heart and brain you will remain.

Here comes the rain again bringing that awful feeling...

Fear comes with pain again, as I lay looking at this ceiling...

Here comes the rain again to me it's once more revealing...

I'm man enough to accept my mistake, my heart is appealing...

This case I have tried over and over again in my mind.

I keep ending up with a guilty verdict each and every time.

I know I'm not an angel, in my closet, skeletons, you can find.

I would be doing life in prison if hurting you was a crime.

I am the judge, jury, and the defendant, so tell me why.

I keep finding myself at fault no matter how I try.

I didn't mean to hurt you, to protect your feelings I would lie.

Now I stand in the rain and hope it hides my tears as I cry.

Here comes the rain again bringing that awful feeling...

Fear comes with pain again, as I lay looking at the ceiling...

Here comes the rain again to me it's once more revealing...

I'm man enough to accept my mistake, my heart is appealing...

o That Feeling *o*

"That feeling" keeps coming back to me like a sad love song.

Why did you have to leave, why did I do you wrong?

It's the truth, it hurts like a bad tooth, like a migraine.

It hurts the heart and strains the brain, I can't sustain or maintain, this pain is hard to contain.

Am I dreaming wide awake? No fake.

I can't take "that feeling" much more, for sure.

I want to come get you, with some rope and duct tape.

You broke my heart, and you don't even have that much of a good shape.

I still adore you, but I curse you, guess it's just a case of "a sour grape".

So, I silently said it, no edit.

I really love you so badly.

Do you trust me? I want no credit.

I really love you so badly.

I don't need you though but it's like I’m facing insanity

Me without you is like a crime against humanity.

I still have all your pictures and your postcards that you sent.

Forever loving me, that's what you said was your intent.

The good times we had at length were times well spent.

Your scent, your strength, a lot to me you meant.

Those eyes, wishing you were here.

Daydreaming that we were both sitting together smiling at each other in a chair.

Mmmmm!!! That smell of your hair, your stare.

I was speaking soft words but you couldn't hear.

I reached over to whisper in your ear, but you vanished in thin air

So, I silently said it, no edit.

I really love you so badly.

Do you trust me? I want no credit.

I really love you so badly.

I feel like I am going crazy, and that is no lie, I am not shy to try.

Then I wonder why, I look up to the sky.

Ok here is the truth "badman" don't cry.

So, I stand in the rain to hide the tears in my eyes.

I was doing very well until I saw you the other day.

I thought I was strong, I thought my feelings for you had gone.

I thought it was over and done, now it's like they are reborn.

No joke, no fun, it has just begun, I had this feeling, butterflies.

Despite my tries, no lies, I wanted to say "hi", but the words just wouldn't come out.

So, I silently said it, no edit.

I really love you so badly.

Do you trust me? No credit.

I really love you so badly.

 # Lost in Emotions #

When your lover cheats it's a sinking feeling of a ''Titanic'' proportion.

Especially when you know you have given them all of your devotion.

It gets deep into your skin like lotion, when someone else gets the promotion.

Just a simple ''wave'' and they are ready to ''splash it out'' like the ocean.

It makes your life standstill, or it's like your world is moving in slow motion.

That's when the simplest of things will always cause a huge commotion.

Because it really hurts to get nil and someone else gets your portion.

And you are expected to take it with a smile, oh what a silly notion.

Lost in emotions, a broken heart is no fun, should I stay or run.

Should I try hard to fix my relationship, although I am still stunned.

Lost in emotions, hungry for love even though I got so much ‘’bun’’.

Feels like I want to grab a gun, put away my misery, now it’s all done.

It hurts to know the smiling face was a facade, it was just a mask,

Mascara to cover all the deceit and hurt for which you did not ask.

You can never again look at that face with trust, it's too tedious a task.

You’re sitting on a stool drowning your sorrows, ordering another flask,

Crying deep inside as you sit and reminisce on the memories of the past.

All the time you invested and tried your best but it just could not last.

How could you not see it coming, were you too naive and moving too fast?

Now your heart is in pieces, victim of an emotional bomb blast.

Lost in emotions, a broken heart is no fun, should I stay or run.

Should I try hard to fix my relationship, although I am still stunned?

Lost in emotions, hungry for love even though I got so much ‘’bun’’.

Feels like I want to grab a gun, put away my misery, now it’s all done.

Emotional Anti-virus

I wish I could find an antivirus to block this feeling like it was spam.

Memories of you keep popping up in my head and make me want to call.

I may act tough on the outside but defenseless on the inside I am.

Your memories are like a virus and to block them I need a firewall.

I will be in the middle of playing a competitive football game.

And all of a sudden thought of you just pop up in my brain,

Even when I am working, trying to make ends meet it's the same.

Embedded in my mind and my heart you are like a permanent stain.

I always seem to think about you continuously when I am
with someone else.

I try to put up a resistance, but my defense is like fire to ice
as it melts.

It seems we were predestined and fated to be together like
Horus and Osiris.

You hacked into my feelings and emotions, now I need an
antivirus.

I wish I could find an antivirus to block this feeling like it
was spam.

Memories of you keep popping up in my head and make me
want to call.

I may act tough on the outside but defenseless on the inside I
am.

Your memories are like a virus and to block them I need a
firewall.

My brain is bombarded with thoughts of ''what if'', ''when''
and ''where''.

Even though we are yesterday's news I must admit without
fear, I still do care.

My emotions are under siege like the city that's in the middle of a war.

I try to run, I try to hide, from your memories I never seem to get too far.

''Old fire sticks'' burn easily, ours would blaze like a furnace if we were near.

It's hard to bear especially with these happy memories that we both share.

Our feelings remain relatively close to each other even when physically we are far.

These feelings need protection from an anti-virus more powerful than an avatar.

I wish I could find an antivirus to block this feeling like it was spam.

Memories of you keep popping up in my head and make me want to call.

I may act tough on the outside but defenseless on the inside I am.

Your memories are like a virus and to block them I need a firewall.

o¥o Gray Skies o¥o

All these memories keep coming back…

I try to keep focused, staying on track…

It's a fact that in my life you had an impact…

Now you are gone, my skies are gray, my clouds are black…

Since you've been gone it's like I lost a piece of me.

I don't know where to find any joy recently.

I keep asking why did you have to leave?

So soon, too soon, I still can't believe it.

I still remember that day we said goodbye.

CHRONICLES OF A BROKEN HEART

If tears can bring you back, I will forever cry.

I remember that final bright sunny afternoon.

Forever my life is gray, darker than a night sky with no moon.

All these memories keep coming back…

I try to keep focused, stay on track…

It's a fact that in my life you had an impact…

Now you are gone, my skies are gray, my clouds are black…

We all miss you, I know you hear our cries.

You are missed by me, myself and I, oh how time flies.

It is a very hard loss to take, but here is our goodbyes.

As we sit and reminisce, looking at these gray skies.

Lots of words unsaid, things we never got to do.

So true, if only I knew, after all we've been through.

It's so sad that one day I would end up losing you.

I never got to say to you, friends like you are very few.

All these memories keep coming back.

I try to keep focused, stay on track.

It's a fact that in my life you had an impact.

Now you are gone, my skies are gray, my clouds are black.

***(For all who lost a loved one) ***

<+> Sunny Days <+>

Sunny days are here again.

I can see clearly now the rain is gone.

I share joy, I no longer fear the pain.

Hark the herald a new person is born.

I am redesigned, call me the "renaissance man".

I am ready for the obstacles of the world.

Bring it on, I will overcome each and every last one.

I won't fall for vanity, or for your pretty girl.

I know beauty is skin deep, some people don’t agree.

The soul is far more beautiful than eyes could ever see.

I won't settle for less; I will be all that I can be.

There are no more dark clouds, the sun now shines for me.

Sunny days are here again.

I can see clearly now the rain is gone.

I share joy, I no longer fear the pain.

Hark the herald a new person is born.

Life is a blessing, to yourself always try to be true.

Sometimes things will not be done the way you planned to do.

You may need a fresh start, never be afraid to start anew.

It will rain sometimes; the sun will not always shine for you.

Life is more for living, than for the things that money pays.

People have different ways of doing things, very funny ways.

They say money talks for them but I never hear what money says.

My life is not about material things

So, I enjoy sunny days.

Sunny days are here again.

I can see clearly now the rain is gone.

I share joy, I no longer fear the pain.

Hark the herald a new person is born.

ooo I Still Wait ooo

I know you are long gone and I should move on...

But I still wait ...

You are relaxing, while I can't get my groove on...

Because I wait...

Maybe you are moving too slow, or I am moving too fast...

But for you I wait...

I am your future but to me you are the past...

But I still wait...

I still wait for you because without you I can't grow...

Just so you know, thoughts of you won't go...

They will never ever be erased; they won't go away...

Deja vu, and flashbacks, games in my mind they play...

Sometimes I know you are near; I feel your presence...

That's why I wait...

You are a part of me, I hold you dear, in every essence...

That's why I wait...

I know that one day you will return to me I am sure...

Until then I wait...

I am lovesick and still I await "true love", the only cure...

Until then I wait...

I still wait for you because without you I can't grow...

Just so you know, thoughts of you won't go...

They will never ever be erased; they won't go away...

Deja vu, and flashbacks, games in my mind they play...

(For all those who still await the return of true love we wait together) ...

@ Give A Little More *@*

You may have had your heart broken and thrown to the floor.

The sun cannot shine in on you if you don't open a window or a door.

Let go of the past even though the future may be unsure.

Leave memories behind of the bad things that happened before.

I don't need material things even though I may be poor.

All I ask is that you give a little love, some time, some more.

You may have been hurt by others in your life before.

So now you only have feelings of resentment in store.

Give a little more and this time I promise you won't get hurt.

You won't see your feelings being trod on and treated like dirt.

You will experience a feeling that you never had since your birth.

Finally, someone is there who acknowledges your worth.

Give some time, some love and don't be afraid to care.

Love is a wonderful thing, so don't be afraid to share.

Give a little more, overcome all mistrust and all fear.

When you reach out for me, I will wipe away each tear.

Even when you are down and out, and life seems unfair.

Troubles may come and it seems like it's too much to bear.

When happiness seems like a distant memory, I will be near.

No matter the situation, for you, I will always be there.

Give a little more and this time I promise you won't get hurt.

You won't see your feelings being trod on and treated like dirt.

You will experience a feeling that you never had since your birth.

Finally, someone is there who acknowledges your worth.

A> Crying In The Rain *>A*.

The past sometimes leaves you with an emotional scar.

Materialistic love will never reach too far.

It's not about all the hype, the bling and the car.

It's about what's on the inside, true love for who you are.

Jealousy and mistrust can lead to a lover's war.

But that's how life goes, you don't always get what you want.

Situations escalate trying to stop but you can't.

Now it's too late, heartache, but you reap what you plant.

I see you crying in the rain...

In your eyes I see the pain...

Things will never be the same...

We don't know who to blame...

Hush baby girl and don't let me see you cry.

Because I won't be affected by the tears in your eyes.

Yes, I played your games and I absorbed every lie.

I just couldn't believe that you had another guy.

I was too blinded by love to see no matter how hard I try.

Suicidal thoughts, no, I rather live and hate you than love you and die.

Now you know why I never looked back on that day I said goodbye.

Situations escalate but now it's time to elevate, spread my wings and fly.

I see you crying in the rain...

In your eyes I see the pain...

Things will never be the same...

We don't know who to blame...

CHRONICLES OF A BROKEN HEART

Sad memories sometimes bring tears.

Relationships torn apart by cheap love affairs.

Sometimes when you called, girl I was never there.

To the word in the street, you gave a listening ear.

I can't say I never cheated, that wouldn't be fair.

We both made mistakes and acted like we didn't care.

There is a special emotional bond that we both share.

Yet still we gave up on the one thing that got us here.

…True Love…

: Broken * Pieces *:*

Gee Free Spirit:

I'm broken, my heart aches at the thought of my parents actually loving me.

I was 12-year-old when I ran away from home, laying my head on the hard cold concrete was better than watching my mum drink away my father's infidelity.

Eating garbage from trash cans, tidying in the local gas station's bathroom is better.

Better than watching them start World War 3 over baby powder.

"There's no place like home" said the Ruby shoe girl, but who would want to leave a place where you have loving and supportive friends on the streets to go home to face "the beasts".

Twenty years later and I still reminisce on my past life not knowing if it's better now or worse.

My life is broken, it's like a curse…

Broken pieces, not knowing what peace is, the pain it eases…

The need to cease it, please release it, the pain increases…

Try to seize it, ego you please it, this game, who sees it…

Deep down beneath it, elitist, you cheat it, more broken pieces…

Juvie:

Wandering around like a stray cat, survival is my only option, my only choice.

My voice is lost, lost among the many voices of the world, so many more of my kind are out there.

Lost and disillusioned by so-called parents who play no part but to destroy your confidence.

Beating you down physically daily, mentally it's even worse, you can't ever be what they expect of you.

Standards even they failed to live up to but now it's like they want to live their life through you.

Not knowing that their "good old days" are but a distant memory, and times have changed, it's a "new you" and people are different from back then.

The pressure is so great, you either make it or you crack and become "broken".

My life is my story, my glory, words unspoken…

Broken pieces, not knowing what peace is, the pain it eases…

The need to cease it, please release it, the pain increases…

Try to seize it, ego you please it, this game, who sees it…

Deep down beneath it, elitist, you cheat it, more broken pieces…

that's what she said.

..."SHE SAID"...

"Love at first sight", been there and done that before.

Only to realize that you could be a psychopathic stalker.

A false pretender with an ulterior motive and more.

So, I won't be impressed by your words "smooth talker".

Yeah, I know I have "beautiful eyes", I heard it all before.

Thanks for the compliment, but a lot of people say the same.

But that said, it has an impact on my mind, yeah sure.

But my heart still refuses to be a part of your emotional game.

Yeah yeah, I know "you love me", yeah whatever...

Words don't have much of an impact on me, but, however...

If you try your best to translate your words into actions...

It just might complete the puzzle of my heart's repair from fractions...

The words you speak cannot substitute for the things you do.

I will judge your actions and not what you say.

Your actions will be your representation if indeed you are true.

What is in the dark will emerge to light, like night is to the day.

Words of seduction and deception, to me it's nothing new.

All for a night of pleasure, to have me as you may.

I am more than just a piece of flesh, and in case you never knew.

I won't be an "object" of your desire, in this game you play.

Yeah yeah, I know "you love me", yeah whatever...

Words don't have much of an impact on me, but, however...

If you try your best and translate your words into actions...

It just might complete the puzzle of my heart's repair from fractions...

So many ways and means, the same objective to achieve.

Spending time and money, everything seems so grand.

Then you always find a reason to leave just as I start to believe.

And then "relationship" becomes a "couple months stand".

To get with me, I know, every means you will conceive.

Sweet seductive words, waving about like a magic wand.

All the gifts and presents and presence the mind can perceive.

Mission accomplished, now it's like you reside in a distant land.

Yeah yeah, I know "you love me", yeah whatever...

Words don't have much impact on me, but, however...

If you try your best to translate your words into actions...

It just might complete the puzzle of my heart's repair from fractions...

*: * Closure *: *

Uncertainty in my head, mental rollercoaster, but this is no form of fun.

A sinister plot, a web of deception that was deliberately spun.

Nowhere to hide from my innermost thoughts, no matter how far I run.

Memories inside, disconsolate feelings in my heart weighing a tonne.

I tried to ignore the echoes of your voice in my ear but I couldn't shun.

I tried to avoid this yearning to come see you, but still I had to come.

All I seek is a reason why you did what you did but you never gave none.
You owe me that much, although the pain and hurt can never be undone.

But still…

I keep fighting emotional battles daily like a soldier…
Trying my best not to fail the test, holding my composure…
Knowing that what we had was great but now it's all over..
I don't need your sympathy; all I seek is just closure…

The whats, the whys, the wheres, the whens, I need to know the hows.
It seems it didn't mean much to you when we were exchanging those vows.
Vows of commitment and trust, all those smiles replaced with frowns.
After all we've been through, struggles and triumphs, you went out of bounds.
There's no more outrage at this stage, face paint, compared to clowns.
Round of applause, encore, the foundation we built, tearing it down.
That was your doing, you ruined, what we had just to be the talk of the town.
I just need to close this chapter, I'm ready please tell me now.

Until then…

I keep fighting emotional battles daily like a soldier…
Trying my best not to fail the test, holding my composure…
Knowing that what we had was great but now it's all over..
I don't need your sympathy; all I seek is just closure…

Anything that has a beginning should most likely have an end.
My friend, we don't even have to talk in person or try to make amends.
Just put my heart at ease by letting me know, if it's even a message you can send.
I'm not seeking reconciliation; I just need to know what happened.
I can live without your presence, it's all good, I'm like an adapter.
We can both move on with our separate lives from here on after.
Living our lives as we choose, enjoying all the fun and all the laughter.
All I need from this story of our lives, is that we close this final chapter.

For now…

I keep fighting emotional battles daily like a soldier…
Trying my best not to fail the test, holding my composure…
Knowing that what we had was great but now it's all over..
I don't need your sympathy; all I seek is just closure…

(((*BONUS*)))

*! * Writing On the wall *! *

It's the real deal, no more limited version or probationary period, the trial is over.

Wake up and smell the roses and face reality, no more mirage, living in denial is over.

This is as real as it gets, reality finally sinking in, "we" are no longer an item.

The burden of sorrow is in the past, the weight of expectations is lightened.

I'm glad to get rid of your gossiping friends and what they used to say about each other.

No more being that guy you wanted me to be, no more family reunions with your mother.

What will you say when she asks for me, I hope it will be the straight truth.
Tell her I cheated and you did the same thing, we were both wrong, no scapegoat.

The writings on the wall and it's plain to see, as clear as a midsummer noon...
It's time to move on to better things, break free from this cocoon...
Disregarding what people say, some say move on, some say it's too soon...
No longer accepting your calls, moving on, after all, the writing is on the wall…

We both did wrong yet still you tried to make it seem like you did it just to get revenge.
Being angry and giving yourself to some friend who doesn't like me makes no sense.
I did it because I yielded to temptation, it wasn't some preconceived intent.
You went all out, lingerie, candles, so intense, burning me while burning incense.
The clear difference, I was weak and fell, while all along you were just in pretense.

If I had an issue, I would have discussed it or just split,
cheating is no defense.
Actually, you doing the same thing is no better than me, the
reason is of no essence.
Cheated to hurt me instead of making a call, made your bed
now lie in it, look at the wall.

The writings on the wall and it's plain to see, as clear as a
midsummer noon...
It's time to move on to better things, break free from this
cocoon...
Disregarding what people say, some say move on, some say
it's too soon...
No longer accepting your calls, moving on, after all, the
writing is on the wall…

Don't think I'm trying to excuse what I did because I won't, it
was a bad mistake.
I'm not hurt because of what you did but it's because
everything you said was fake.
You always swore you were so in love with me you couldn't
have eyes for another guy.

Yet in the blink of an eye, you found someone to cheat with,
without him having to try.
It's obvious that he was there all along, maybe it's not a
onetime thing, it was a clear plan.
It's hard to see where the person you have that much trust in,
suddenly appears from.
It seems like you have been playing from the beginning, you
were as smooth as silk.
I played and have been played, my dues have now been paid,
I'm not crying over spilt milk.

The writings on the wall and it's plain to see, as clear as a
midsummer noon...
It's time to move on to better things, break free from this
cocoon...
Disregarding what people say, some say move on, some say
it's too soon...
No longer accepting your calls, moving on, after all, the
writing is on the wall…

ABOUT THE AUTHOR

Jamaican born Evol Dillon is the author of the book *Chronicles Of A Broken Heart.* A native of the town of Linstead, St. Catherine he attended Charlemont High School, before moving on to Jose Marti Technical High School.

He then relocated to Portmore, St. Catherine and attended Excelsior Community College where he pursued a course in Electrical Technology.

He also holds a certificate in Telemarketing and also in Customer Relations.

While attending Excelsior Community College he began playing semi-professional soccer, representing Greater Portmore United soccer team.

During this stint he won numerous awards and went to become captain of the team for a span of over 10 years.

After getting injured during one of his many trials and being home for an extended period that was when reality struck that maybe his dream of becoming a professional soccer player wasn't going to become a reality.

He got employed as a Stores Handyman at the Jamaican Urban Transit Company, during a tenure that lasted 20 years he went on to serve as Stores Clerk, he also worked as Stores Supervisor at depot level and also at the Central Stores located at the Head Office.

During this time, he also represented the company in soccer for a period of 20 years, 15 of which he was the team captain.

He also represented Dunbeholden F.C in the Division one, Major League and Super League.

A kindhearted and very jovial person, he is known throughout his community for his charitable efforts and contributions to assisting the needy and helping many youths gaining employment and mentoring them.

Made in the USA
Columbia, SC
25 March 2025

55667999R10098